50 Pot Dinners for Home

By: Kelly Johnson

Table of Contents

- Beef Stew
- Chicken and Rice
- Vegetable Soup
- Chicken Pot Pie
- Pork Carnitas
- Chili Con Carne
- Beef and Mushroom Stroganoff
- Chicken Alfredo
- Baked Ziti
- Shepherd's Pie
- Spaghetti Bolognese
- Seafood Gumbo
- Beef and Vegetable Casserole
- Chicken and Dumplings
- Jambalaya
- Meatball Soup
- Beef Ragu
- Slow Cooker Chili
- Sausage and Peppers
- Beef and Barley Soup
- Creamy Chicken and Spinach Pasta
- Chicken Tikka Masala
- Moroccan Lamb Stew
- Lentil Soup
- Chicken and Sausage Gumbo
- Shrimp and Grits
- Chicken and Sweet Potato Curry
- Braised Short Ribs
- Chicken Enchilada Casserole
- Pulled Pork Sandwiches
- Chicken Fried Rice
- Beef and Potato Hash
- Chicken Parmesan
- Stuffed Bell Peppers
- Teriyaki Chicken and Veggies

- Pot Roast
- Chicken Fajitas
- Beef and Vegetable Stir Fry
- Slow Cooker Pot Roast
- Stuffed Cabbage Rolls
- Chicken and Sausage Paella
- Shrimp Scampi Pasta
- Beef Wellington Casserole
- Turkey Chili
- Ratatouille
- Beef and Cheese Taco Skillet
- Chicken Marsala
- Sausage and Sauerkraut
- Beef Burrito Bowls
- Chicken and Rice Casserole

Beef Stew

Ingredients:

- 1 lb beef stew meat, cubed
- 4 cups beef broth
- 2 medium carrots, sliced
- 2 medium potatoes, diced
- 1 onion, chopped
- 2 cloves garlic, minced
- 2 tablespoons flour
- 1 tablespoon tomato paste
- 1 teaspoon dried thyme
- 1 teaspoon dried rosemary
- Salt and pepper to taste
- 2 tablespoons olive oil
- 1 cup frozen peas (optional)

Instructions:

1. Heat olive oil in a large pot over medium-high heat. Brown the beef stew meat in batches, then remove and set aside.
2. Add onions and garlic to the pot, cooking until softened, about 3 minutes.
3. Sprinkle flour over the onions and garlic, stirring to coat. Cook for another minute to form a roux.
4. Stir in the tomato paste, beef broth, thyme, rosemary, salt, and pepper. Bring to a simmer.
5. Add the browned beef, carrots, and potatoes. Cover and simmer on low for about 1.5 to 2 hours, or until the meat is tender.
6. Add frozen peas in the last 10 minutes of cooking, if desired.
7. Taste and adjust seasoning before serving.

Chicken and Rice

Ingredients:

- 2 cups chicken broth
- 1 cup long-grain white rice
- 2 chicken breasts, boneless and skinless, cut into cubes
- 1 onion, chopped
- 2 cloves garlic, minced
- 1 teaspoon dried thyme
- 1 teaspoon paprika
- Salt and pepper to taste
- 2 tablespoons olive oil
- 1/2 cup frozen peas (optional)
- Fresh parsley for garnish (optional)

Instructions:

1. Heat olive oil in a large skillet over medium heat. Add chicken cubes and cook until browned and cooked through, about 5-7 minutes. Remove and set aside.
2. In the same skillet, add onions and garlic. Sauté until softened, about 3 minutes.
3. Add rice and toast for 1-2 minutes.
4. Pour in chicken broth, thyme, paprika, salt, and pepper. Bring to a simmer, cover, and cook for 15-20 minutes, or until rice is tender and liquid is absorbed.
5. Stir in cooked chicken and frozen peas, if using. Cover and let sit for 5 minutes before serving.
6. Garnish with fresh parsley if desired.

Vegetable Soup

Ingredients:

- 1 tablespoon olive oil
- 1 onion, chopped
- 2 cloves garlic, minced
- 2 carrots, diced
- 2 celery stalks, diced
- 2 potatoes, diced
- 1 zucchini, chopped
- 1 can diced tomatoes (14.5 oz)
- 4 cups vegetable broth
- 1 teaspoon dried thyme
- Salt and pepper to taste
- 1 cup frozen green beans
- 1 cup spinach or kale (optional)

Instructions:

1. Heat olive oil in a large pot over medium heat. Add onion and garlic, cooking until softened.
2. Add carrots, celery, potatoes, and zucchini, and sauté for 5 minutes.
3. Stir in diced tomatoes, vegetable broth, thyme, salt, and pepper. Bring to a boil.
4. Reduce heat and simmer for 30 minutes or until vegetables are tender.
5. Add green beans and spinach (if using) and cook for an additional 5 minutes.
6. Taste and adjust seasoning before serving.

Chicken Pot Pie

Ingredients:

- 2 cups cooked, shredded chicken
- 1 cup frozen mixed vegetables (peas, carrots, corn)
- 1/2 cup milk
- 1/2 cup chicken broth
- 1/3 cup all-purpose flour
- 1/4 cup butter
- 1 onion, chopped
- 1/2 teaspoon garlic powder
- Salt and pepper to taste
- 1 package refrigerated pie crusts (or homemade)
- 1 egg, beaten (for egg wash)

Instructions:

1. Preheat the oven to 425°F (220°C).
2. In a large skillet, melt butter over medium heat. Add onions and cook until soft.
3. Stir in flour and cook for 1-2 minutes to form a roux.
4. Gradually add chicken broth and milk, whisking constantly to avoid lumps. Simmer until thickened, about 5 minutes.
5. Stir in shredded chicken, mixed vegetables, garlic powder, salt, and pepper. Cook for an additional 5 minutes.
6. Roll out pie crust and line a pie dish. Pour the chicken mixture into the crust.
7. Cover with a second pie crust and crimp the edges. Cut a few slits in the top to allow steam to escape.
8. Brush the top with a beaten egg for a golden crust.
9. Bake for 30-35 minutes, or until golden brown. Let cool for a few minutes before serving.

Pork Carnitas

Ingredients:

- 2 lb pork shoulder, cut into chunks
- 1 onion, chopped
- 4 cloves garlic, minced
- 1 orange, juiced
- 1 lime, juiced
- 1 tablespoon chili powder
- 1 teaspoon cumin
- 1 teaspoon oregano
- Salt and pepper to taste
- 1/2 cup chicken broth
- 2 tablespoons olive oil
- Tortillas and toppings (for serving)

Instructions:

1. In a slow cooker, combine pork shoulder, onion, garlic, orange juice, lime juice, chili powder, cumin, oregano, salt, and pepper.
2. Pour in chicken broth and stir to combine.
3. Cover and cook on low for 8 hours or until the pork is tender and easily shreds.
4. Remove the pork and shred with two forks.
5. Heat olive oil in a skillet over medium-high heat. Add shredded pork and cook until crispy and browned, about 5-7 minutes.
6. Serve with tortillas and your favorite toppings (like cilantro, salsa, and avocado).

Chili Con Carne

Ingredients:

- 1 lb ground beef
- 1 onion, chopped
- 2 cloves garlic, minced
- 1 can diced tomatoes (14.5 oz)
- 1 can kidney beans, drained and rinsed
- 1 can black beans, drained and rinsed
- 1 tablespoon chili powder
- 1 teaspoon cumin
- 1/2 teaspoon paprika
- Salt and pepper to taste
- 1 cup beef broth
- 1/2 cup shredded cheddar cheese (optional)
- Sour cream for topping (optional)

Instructions:

1. In a large pot, brown ground beef over medium heat. Remove excess fat.
2. Add onions and garlic, and sauté until softened.
3. Stir in diced tomatoes, kidney beans, black beans, chili powder, cumin, paprika, salt, pepper, and beef broth.
4. Bring to a boil, then reduce heat and simmer for 30 minutes, stirring occasionally.
5. Serve with shredded cheese and sour cream, if desired.

Beef and Mushroom Stroganoff

Ingredients:

- 1 lb beef sirloin or stew meat, thinly sliced
- 8 oz mushrooms, sliced
- 1 onion, chopped
- 2 cloves garlic, minced
- 1 cup beef broth
- 1/2 cup sour cream
- 1 tablespoon flour
- 2 tablespoons olive oil
- 1 teaspoon Worcestershire sauce
- Salt and pepper to taste
- Egg noodles (for serving)

Instructions:

1. Heat olive oil in a large skillet over medium-high heat. Brown the beef slices and remove from the skillet.
2. In the same skillet, sauté onions, garlic, and mushrooms until softened.
3. Stir in flour and cook for 1-2 minutes.
4. Add beef broth, Worcestershire sauce, and salt and pepper. Bring to a simmer.
5. Return the beef to the skillet and cook for 5-7 minutes until the sauce thickens.
6. Stir in sour cream and cook for an additional 2 minutes.
7. Serve over cooked egg noodles.

Chicken Alfredo

Ingredients:

- 2 boneless, skinless chicken breasts
- 1 tablespoon olive oil
- 3 cloves garlic, minced
- 1 cup heavy cream
- 1/2 cup grated Parmesan cheese
- 1/2 teaspoon dried basil
- Salt and pepper to taste
- 8 oz fettuccine pasta
- Fresh parsley for garnish

Instructions:

1. Heat olive oil in a skillet over medium heat. Season chicken breasts with salt and pepper, then cook until browned and cooked through, about 6-7 minutes per side. Remove and slice thinly.
2. Cook the fettuccine pasta according to package instructions, then drain and set aside.
3. In the same skillet, add garlic and sauté for 1-2 minutes.
4. Stir in heavy cream, Parmesan cheese, basil, salt, and pepper. Simmer for 5 minutes or until the sauce thickens.
5. Add the cooked pasta to the sauce and toss to coat.
6. Serve with sliced chicken on top and garnish with fresh parsley.

Baked Ziti

Ingredients:

- 1 lb ziti pasta
- 2 cups marinara sauce
- 1 lb ground beef or Italian sausage
- 1 onion, chopped
- 2 cloves garlic, minced
- 1 teaspoon dried basil
- 1 teaspoon dried oregano
- Salt and pepper to taste
- 2 cups ricotta cheese
- 1 egg
- 2 cups shredded mozzarella cheese
- 1/2 cup grated Parmesan cheese

Instructions:

1. Preheat the oven to 375°F (190°C).
2. Cook the ziti pasta according to package instructions. Drain and set aside.
3. In a large skillet, brown the ground beef or sausage with onions and garlic. Drain any excess fat.
4. Stir in marinara sauce, basil, oregano, salt, and pepper. Simmer for 10 minutes.
5. In a mixing bowl, combine ricotta cheese, egg, 1 cup of mozzarella, and Parmesan cheese. Stir to combine.
6. In a baking dish, layer half of the cooked ziti, then half of the meat sauce, and half of the cheese mixture. Repeat the layers.
7. Top with the remaining mozzarella cheese and bake for 25-30 minutes, or until bubbly and golden brown.
8. Let cool for a few minutes before serving.

Shepherd's Pie

Ingredients:

- 1 lb ground beef or lamb
- 1 onion, chopped
- 2 carrots, diced
- 1 cup peas (frozen or fresh)
- 2 cloves garlic, minced
- 1 tablespoon Worcestershire sauce
- 1/4 cup beef broth
- 1 teaspoon dried thyme
- Salt and pepper to taste
- 4 cups mashed potatoes (prepared)
- 2 tablespoons butter (for topping)

Instructions:

1. Preheat the oven to 400°F (200°C).
2. In a large skillet, brown the ground beef or lamb with onions, carrots, and garlic.
3. Stir in Worcestershire sauce, beef broth, peas, thyme, salt, and pepper. Simmer for 5-7 minutes.
4. Transfer the meat mixture to a greased baking dish. Spread mashed potatoes over the top, smoothing it out with a spatula.
5. Dot the top with butter and bake for 20-25 minutes, or until the top is golden and slightly crispy.
6. Let sit for 5 minutes before serving.

Spaghetti Bolognese

Ingredients:

- 1 lb ground beef or pork
- 1 onion, chopped
- 2 cloves garlic, minced
- 1 carrot, grated
- 1 celery stalk, chopped
- 1 can crushed tomatoes (14.5 oz)
- 1 tablespoon tomato paste
- 1 teaspoon dried oregano
- 1 teaspoon dried basil
- Salt and pepper to taste
- 1/2 cup red wine (optional)
- 1 lb spaghetti pasta
- Fresh parsley for garnish

Instructions:

1. Cook the spaghetti pasta according to package instructions. Drain and set aside.
2. In a large skillet, brown the ground meat with onions, garlic, carrot, and celery.
3. Stir in tomato paste, crushed tomatoes, oregano, basil, salt, and pepper. If using, add red wine and simmer for 30 minutes.
4. Serve the Bolognese sauce over the cooked spaghetti.
5. Garnish with fresh parsley before serving.

Seafood Gumbo

Ingredients:

- 1 lb shrimp, peeled and deveined
- 1/2 lb crab meat
- 1/2 lb sausage, sliced (andouille sausage recommended)
- 1 onion, chopped
- 1 bell pepper, chopped
- 2 celery stalks, chopped
- 2 cloves garlic, minced
- 4 cups chicken broth
- 1 can diced tomatoes (14.5 oz)
- 1/4 cup flour
- 1/4 cup vegetable oil
- 1 teaspoon thyme
- 1 teaspoon paprika
- 1 teaspoon cayenne pepper
- Salt and pepper to taste
- 1/4 cup parsley, chopped
- Cooked rice (for serving)

Instructions:

1. In a large pot, make a roux by combining flour and oil over medium heat. Stir continuously until the mixture turns a dark brown, about 10 minutes.
2. Add onions, bell pepper, celery, and garlic. Sauté until softened, about 5 minutes.
3. Stir in chicken broth, tomatoes, thyme, paprika, cayenne, salt, and pepper. Bring to a boil.
4. Lower the heat and simmer for 30 minutes, stirring occasionally.
5. Add shrimp, crab meat, and sausage to the gumbo. Cook for another 5-7 minutes, until the shrimp is cooked through.
6. Serve over cooked rice and garnish with parsley.

Beef and Vegetable Casserole

Ingredients:

- 1 lb ground beef
- 1 onion, chopped
- 2 carrots, chopped
- 1 cup frozen peas
- 1 cup corn kernels
- 1 can cream of mushroom soup (10.5 oz)
- 1/2 cup milk
- 1 1/2 cups shredded cheddar cheese
- Salt and pepper to taste
- 4 cups mashed potatoes (prepared)

Instructions:

1. Preheat the oven to 350°F (175°C).
2. In a large skillet, brown the ground beef with onions. Drain any excess fat.
3. Stir in carrots, peas, corn, mushroom soup, milk, and cheddar cheese. Season with salt and pepper and cook for 5 minutes.
4. Transfer the beef mixture to a greased baking dish. Spread mashed potatoes over the top.
5. Bake for 25-30 minutes, or until the top is golden and bubbly.
6. Let sit for 5 minutes before serving.

Chicken and Dumplings

Ingredients:

- 1 lb chicken breasts, cooked and shredded
- 1 onion, chopped
- 2 carrots, diced
- 2 celery stalks, chopped
- 4 cups chicken broth
- 1 can cream of chicken soup (10.5 oz)
- 2 teaspoons dried thyme
- Salt and pepper to taste
- 2 cups biscuit mix
- 2/3 cup milk
- 2 tablespoons butter

Instructions:

1. In a large pot, combine chicken broth, cream of chicken soup, onions, carrots, celery, thyme, salt, and pepper. Bring to a boil and simmer for 15 minutes.
2. Stir in shredded chicken and continue to simmer.
3. In a separate bowl, mix biscuit mix and milk to form dumpling dough.
4. Drop spoonfuls of the dumpling dough into the simmering soup. Cover and cook for 15-20 minutes, or until the dumplings are cooked through.
5. Stir in butter and serve hot.

Jambalaya

Ingredients:

- 1 lb sausage (andouille or smoked sausage)
- 1 lb chicken breast, diced
- 1 bell pepper, chopped
- 1 onion, chopped
- 2 cloves garlic, minced
- 1 can diced tomatoes (14.5 oz)
- 1 1/2 cups rice
- 3 cups chicken broth
- 1 teaspoon thyme
- 1 teaspoon paprika
- 1/2 teaspoon cayenne pepper
- Salt and pepper to taste
- 1/2 lb shrimp, peeled and deveined
- 1/4 cup green onions, chopped

Instructions:

1. In a large pot, brown sausage and chicken over medium heat. Remove and set aside.
2. In the same pot, sauté bell pepper, onion, and garlic until softened.
3. Stir in diced tomatoes, rice, chicken broth, thyme, paprika, cayenne, salt, and pepper. Bring to a boil.
4. Lower the heat, cover, and simmer for 20 minutes.
5. Add shrimp and cook for another 5-7 minutes, until the shrimp is pink and the rice is cooked.
6. Garnish with green onions and serve.

Meatball Soup

Ingredients:

- 1 lb ground beef
- 1/2 cup breadcrumbs
- 1 egg
- 1/4 cup grated Parmesan cheese
- 1 teaspoon dried oregano
- 1 teaspoon garlic powder
- Salt and pepper to taste
- 4 cups beef broth
- 1 can diced tomatoes (14.5 oz)
- 2 carrots, diced
- 1 onion, chopped
- 1 zucchini, chopped
- 1/2 cup pasta (small shapes like orzo or elbow)
- Fresh parsley for garnish

Instructions:

1. In a mixing bowl, combine ground beef, breadcrumbs, egg, Parmesan cheese, oregano, garlic powder, salt, and pepper. Form into small meatballs.
2. In a large pot, bring beef broth and diced tomatoes to a boil. Add meatballs and simmer for 10 minutes.
3. Stir in carrots, onion, zucchini, and pasta. Simmer for another 15-20 minutes, until the vegetables are tender.
4. Serve garnished with fresh parsley.

Beef Ragu

Ingredients:

- 2 lbs beef chuck roast, cut into chunks
- 1 onion, chopped
- 2 cloves garlic, minced
- 1 carrot, chopped
- 1 celery stalk, chopped
- 1 can crushed tomatoes (14.5 oz)
- 1/2 cup red wine (optional)
- 1 teaspoon dried basil
- 1 teaspoon dried oregano
- Salt and pepper to taste
- 1 bay leaf
- 1 cup beef broth
- 1 tablespoon olive oil
- Fresh pasta (like pappardelle or tagliatelle), for serving
- Fresh Parmesan cheese, for garnish

Instructions:

1. In a large pot, heat olive oil over medium heat. Brown beef chunks on all sides, then remove and set aside.
2. Add onion, garlic, carrot, and celery to the pot, sautéing until softened, about 5 minutes.
3. Stir in crushed tomatoes, red wine (if using), basil, oregano, salt, pepper, and bay leaf.
4. Return beef to the pot and add beef broth. Bring to a simmer.
5. Cover and cook for 2-3 hours, or until the beef is tender and can be shredded with a fork.
6. Remove bay leaf and shred the beef. Toss with cooked pasta and serve with Parmesan.

Slow Cooker Chili

Ingredients:

- 1 lb ground beef or turkey
- 1 onion, chopped
- 1 bell pepper, chopped
- 2 cloves garlic, minced
- 1 can diced tomatoes (14.5 oz)
- 1 can kidney beans (14.5 oz), drained and rinsed
- 1 can black beans (14.5 oz), drained and rinsed
- 1 can tomato paste (6 oz)
- 1 tablespoon chili powder
- 1 teaspoon cumin
- 1 teaspoon smoked paprika
- Salt and pepper to taste
- 1/2 cup beef broth or water
- Optional toppings: sour cream, shredded cheese, green onions

Instructions:

1. Brown ground meat in a skillet over medium heat, then transfer to a slow cooker.
2. Add onion, bell pepper, garlic, diced tomatoes, beans, tomato paste, chili powder, cumin, paprika, salt, and pepper.
3. Pour in beef broth and stir everything together.
4. Cover and cook on low for 6-8 hours or high for 3-4 hours.
5. Serve with your favorite chili toppings.

Sausage and Peppers

Ingredients:

- 1 lb Italian sausage (mild or spicy)
- 2 bell peppers, sliced
- 1 onion, sliced
- 2 cloves garlic, minced
- 1 can diced tomatoes (14.5 oz)
- 1 teaspoon dried oregano
- 1 teaspoon dried basil
- Salt and pepper to taste
- Olive oil for sautéing

Instructions:

1. Heat olive oil in a large skillet over medium heat. Brown sausages on all sides, then remove and set aside.
2. In the same skillet, sauté bell peppers, onion, and garlic until softened, about 5 minutes.
3. Slice sausages into bite-sized pieces and return them to the skillet. Add diced tomatoes, oregano, basil, salt, and pepper.
4. Simmer for 15-20 minutes, until the sausages are fully cooked and the flavors meld together.
5. Serve hot with crusty bread or over rice.

Beef and Barley Soup

Ingredients:

- 1 lb beef stew meat, cut into cubes
- 1 onion, chopped
- 2 carrots, diced
- 2 celery stalks, chopped
- 2 cloves garlic, minced
- 1/2 cup pearl barley
- 4 cups beef broth
- 1 can diced tomatoes (14.5 oz)
- 1 teaspoon dried thyme
- Salt and pepper to taste
- 2 tablespoons olive oil

Instructions:

1. Heat olive oil in a large pot over medium heat. Brown beef stew meat on all sides, then remove and set aside.
2. Add onion, carrots, celery, and garlic to the pot, sautéing until softened, about 5 minutes.
3. Stir in beef broth, diced tomatoes, barley, thyme, salt, and pepper. Bring to a boil.
4. Reduce heat and simmer for 1 hour, or until the beef is tender and the barley is cooked.
5. Serve hot, garnished with fresh parsley if desired.

Creamy Chicken and Spinach Pasta

Ingredients:

- 1 lb chicken breast, cut into strips
- 1 tablespoon olive oil
- 2 cloves garlic, minced
- 2 cups spinach, chopped
- 1 cup heavy cream
- 1 cup chicken broth
- 1 teaspoon dried basil
- 1 teaspoon dried oregano
- Salt and pepper to taste
- 1 lb pasta (penne or fettuccine)
- Grated Parmesan cheese for garnish

Instructions:

1. Cook pasta according to package instructions. Drain and set aside.
2. Heat olive oil in a large skillet over medium heat. Cook chicken strips until browned and cooked through, then remove from the pan.
3. In the same skillet, sauté garlic until fragrant. Add spinach and cook until wilted.
4. Stir in heavy cream, chicken broth, basil, oregano, salt, and pepper. Bring to a simmer and cook for 5 minutes.
5. Return chicken to the skillet and add cooked pasta. Toss to combine.
6. Serve with grated Parmesan cheese.

Chicken Tikka Masala

Ingredients:

- 1 lb chicken breast, diced
- 1 cup plain yogurt
- 2 teaspoons garam masala
- 1 teaspoon cumin
- 1 teaspoon turmeric
- 1 teaspoon paprika
- 2 cloves garlic, minced
- 1 onion, chopped
- 1 can diced tomatoes (14.5 oz)
- 1 cup heavy cream
- 1 tablespoon olive oil
- Salt and pepper to taste
- Cooked rice for serving
- Fresh cilantro for garnish

Instructions:

1. Marinate chicken in yogurt, garam masala, cumin, turmeric, paprika, garlic, salt, and pepper for at least 30 minutes.
2. Heat olive oil in a large skillet over medium heat. Sauté onions until softened, about 5 minutes.
3. Add marinated chicken to the skillet and cook until browned and cooked through, about 10 minutes.
4. Stir in diced tomatoes and simmer for 10 minutes. Add heavy cream and continue simmering for another 5 minutes.
5. Serve over cooked rice and garnish with fresh cilantro.

Moroccan Lamb Stew

Ingredients:

- 1 lb lamb stew meat, cut into cubes
- 1 onion, chopped
- 2 cloves garlic, minced
- 1 carrot, sliced
- 1 zucchini, chopped
- 1 can diced tomatoes (14.5 oz)
- 1 cup beef broth
- 1 tablespoon cumin
- 1 teaspoon cinnamon
- 1 teaspoon paprika
- 1/2 teaspoon turmeric
- 1/2 cup dried apricots, chopped
- Salt and pepper to taste
- Olive oil for cooking

Instructions:

1. Heat olive oil in a large pot over medium heat. Brown lamb stew meat on all sides, then remove and set aside.
2. In the same pot, sauté onions and garlic until softened, about 5 minutes.
3. Stir in carrots, zucchini, diced tomatoes, beef broth, cumin, cinnamon, paprika, turmeric, apricots, salt, and pepper.
4. Return lamb to the pot and bring to a simmer. Cook for 1.5-2 hours, or until the lamb is tender.
5. Serve hot with couscous or bread.

Lentil Soup

Ingredients:

- 1 cup dried lentils, rinsed
- 1 onion, chopped
- 2 carrots, diced
- 2 celery stalks, chopped
- 2 cloves garlic, minced
- 1 can diced tomatoes (14.5 oz)
- 4 cups vegetable broth
- 1 teaspoon cumin
- 1/2 teaspoon turmeric
- 1 teaspoon paprika
- Salt and pepper to taste
- Olive oil for sautéing
- Fresh parsley for garnish

Instructions:

1. Heat olive oil in a large pot over medium heat. Sauté onions, carrots, celery, and garlic until softened, about 5 minutes.
2. Stir in lentils, diced tomatoes, vegetable broth, cumin, turmeric, paprika, salt, and pepper.
3. Bring to a boil, then reduce heat and simmer for 30-40 minutes, until lentils are tender.
4. Serve garnished with fresh parsley.

Chicken and Sausage Gumbo

Ingredients:

- 1 lb chicken thighs, boneless and skinless, chopped
- 1 lb smoked sausage, sliced
- 1 onion, chopped
- 1 bell pepper, chopped
- 2 celery stalks, chopped
- 4 cloves garlic, minced
- 1 can diced tomatoes (14.5 oz)
- 6 cups chicken broth
- 1/4 cup flour
- 1/4 cup vegetable oil
- 2 teaspoons paprika
- 1 teaspoon thyme
- 2 bay leaves
- 1 teaspoon Cajun seasoning
- Salt and pepper to taste
- Cooked rice for serving
- Fresh parsley for garnish

Instructions:

1. In a large pot, make a roux by heating oil over medium heat and stirring in flour. Cook, stirring constantly, until the mixture turns dark brown, about 10-15 minutes.
2. Add onion, bell pepper, celery, and garlic to the pot. Cook for 5 minutes until softened.
3. Stir in chicken broth, diced tomatoes, smoked sausage, chicken, paprika, thyme, Cajun seasoning, bay leaves, salt, and pepper.
4. Bring to a simmer and cook for 1-1.5 hours, until the chicken is tender.
5. Serve over cooked rice and garnish with fresh parsley.

Shrimp and Grits

Ingredients:

- 1 lb shrimp, peeled and deveined
- 1 tablespoon olive oil
- 1/2 cup chicken broth
- 2 cloves garlic, minced
- 1 tablespoon lemon juice
- 1/2 teaspoon paprika
- 1/2 teaspoon cayenne pepper
- Salt and pepper to taste
- 1 cup stone-ground grits
- 4 cups water
- 2 tablespoons butter
- 1 cup shredded cheddar cheese

Instructions:

1. In a medium saucepan, bring water to a boil and stir in grits. Lower heat and simmer, stirring frequently, until thickened (about 20 minutes). Stir in butter and cheddar cheese, and season with salt and pepper.
2. In a large skillet, heat olive oil over medium heat. Add shrimp and cook until pink and cooked through, about 4-5 minutes.
3. Remove shrimp from the skillet and set aside. In the same skillet, add chicken broth, garlic, lemon juice, paprika, cayenne, salt, and pepper. Simmer for 2-3 minutes until slightly reduced.
4. Return shrimp to the skillet and toss to coat.
5. Serve shrimp over grits, garnished with parsley if desired.

Chicken and Sweet Potato Curry

Ingredients:

- 1 lb chicken breast, cubed
- 2 medium sweet potatoes, peeled and cubed
- 1 onion, chopped
- 2 cloves garlic, minced
- 1 can coconut milk (14 oz)
- 1 tablespoon curry powder
- 1 teaspoon ground ginger
- 1 teaspoon turmeric
- 1 teaspoon cumin
- 1/2 teaspoon cinnamon
- 2 cups chicken broth
- Salt and pepper to taste
- 2 tablespoons olive oil
- Fresh cilantro for garnish

Instructions:

1. Heat olive oil in a large pot over medium heat. Add chicken and cook until browned, about 5 minutes. Remove and set aside.
2. In the same pot, add onion and garlic and sauté until softened, about 5 minutes.
3. Stir in curry powder, ginger, turmeric, cumin, and cinnamon. Cook for 1-2 minutes to release the spices' aromas.
4. Add sweet potatoes, coconut milk, chicken broth, salt, and pepper. Bring to a simmer and cook for 20-25 minutes, until sweet potatoes are tender.
5. Return chicken to the pot and cook for an additional 5-10 minutes until heated through.
6. Serve hot, garnished with fresh cilantro.

Braised Short Ribs

Ingredients:

- 4 beef short ribs
- 2 tablespoons olive oil
- 1 onion, chopped
- 2 carrots, chopped
- 2 celery stalks, chopped
- 3 cloves garlic, minced
- 2 cups red wine
- 2 cups beef broth
- 1 tablespoon tomato paste
- 2 bay leaves
- 2 teaspoons thyme
- Salt and pepper to taste

Instructions:

1. Preheat the oven to 325°F (163°C).
2. Heat olive oil in a large oven-safe pot over medium heat. Brown the short ribs on all sides, about 5 minutes. Remove and set aside.
3. In the same pot, add onion, carrots, celery, and garlic. Cook until softened, about 5 minutes.
4. Stir in tomato paste, wine, beef broth, bay leaves, thyme, salt, and pepper. Bring to a simmer.
5. Return short ribs to the pot, cover, and transfer to the oven. Braise for 2.5-3 hours, until the meat is tender and falling off the bone.
6. Serve with mashed potatoes or rice, spooning the braising liquid over the ribs.

Chicken Enchilada Casserole

Ingredients:

- 2 cups cooked chicken, shredded
- 1 can enchilada sauce (14 oz)
- 1 can diced green chilies (4 oz)
- 1 onion, chopped
- 1 cup corn kernels
- 1 can black beans, drained and rinsed
- 1 teaspoon cumin
- 1 teaspoon chili powder
- Salt and pepper to taste
- 12 corn tortillas
- 2 cups shredded cheddar cheese
- Fresh cilantro for garnish

Instructions:

1. Preheat the oven to 350°F (175°C).
2. In a large bowl, mix together chicken, enchilada sauce, green chilies, onion, corn, black beans, cumin, chili powder, salt, and pepper.
3. In a 9x13-inch baking dish, layer tortillas, followed by a layer of the chicken mixture, and top with cheese. Repeat layers, finishing with cheese on top.
4. Bake for 25-30 minutes, until bubbly and the cheese is golden brown.
5. Garnish with fresh cilantro and serve hot.

Pulled Pork Sandwiches

Ingredients:

- 3 lb pork shoulder
- 1 tablespoon paprika
- 1 tablespoon brown sugar
- 1 teaspoon salt
- 1 teaspoon black pepper
- 1 teaspoon garlic powder
- 1 teaspoon onion powder
- 1 teaspoon cayenne pepper
- 1 cup barbecue sauce
- 8 hamburger buns
- Coleslaw for topping

Instructions:

1. Preheat the oven to 300°F (150°C).
2. Mix together paprika, brown sugar, salt, pepper, garlic powder, onion powder, and cayenne. Rub this mixture all over the pork shoulder.
3. Place the pork in a roasting pan and cover with foil. Roast for 3-4 hours, or until the pork is fork-tender.
4. Remove pork from the oven and shred with two forks.
5. Toss the shredded pork with barbecue sauce.
6. Serve on hamburger buns, topped with coleslaw.

Chicken Fried Rice

Ingredients:

- 2 cups cooked rice (preferably chilled)
- 2 tablespoons vegetable oil
- 2 chicken breasts, diced
- 1 onion, chopped
- 1 cup frozen peas and carrots
- 3 eggs, beaten
- 3 tablespoons soy sauce
- 2 teaspoons sesame oil
- 2 cloves garlic, minced
- 2 green onions, chopped

Instructions:

1. Heat vegetable oil in a large skillet or wok over medium-high heat. Add chicken and cook until browned, about 5 minutes. Remove and set aside.
2. In the same skillet, add onion, garlic, peas, and carrots. Sauté until softened, about 3 minutes.
3. Push the vegetables to the side and scramble the eggs in the same pan.
4. Add the cooked rice, chicken, soy sauce, and sesame oil. Stir to combine and cook for 5 minutes until heated through.
5. Garnish with green onions and serve hot.

Beef and Potato Hash

Ingredients:

- 1 lb ground beef
- 3 large potatoes, peeled and diced
- 1 onion, chopped
- 1 bell pepper, chopped
- 2 cloves garlic, minced
- 1 teaspoon paprika
- 1/2 teaspoon cumin
- Salt and pepper to taste
- 2 tablespoons vegetable oil
- Fresh parsley for garnish

Instructions:

1. Heat vegetable oil in a large skillet over medium heat. Add ground beef and cook until browned, about 5-7 minutes. Remove and set aside.
2. In the same skillet, add potatoes and cook until browned and crispy, about 10-12 minutes.
3. Add onion, bell pepper, and garlic, and cook until softened, about 5 minutes.
4. Stir in paprika, cumin, salt, pepper, and the cooked ground beef. Cook for another 5 minutes to combine the flavors.
5. Garnish with fresh parsley and serve hot.

Chicken Parmesan

Ingredients:

- 4 boneless, skinless chicken breasts
- 1 cup breadcrumbs
- 1/2 cup grated Parmesan cheese
- 1 teaspoon garlic powder
- 1 teaspoon Italian seasoning
- 2 eggs, beaten
- 2 cups marinara sauce
- 2 cups shredded mozzarella cheese
- 2 tablespoons olive oil
- Salt and pepper to taste
- Fresh basil for garnish

Instructions:

1. Preheat the oven to 375°F (190°C).
2. In a shallow dish, mix breadcrumbs, Parmesan cheese, garlic powder, Italian seasoning, salt, and pepper.
3. Dip each chicken breast in beaten eggs, then coat with the breadcrumb mixture, pressing gently to adhere.
4. Heat olive oil in a large ovenproof skillet over medium heat. Cook the chicken breasts for 2-3 minutes per side, until golden brown.
5. Spoon marinara sauce over the chicken and top with mozzarella cheese.
6. Transfer the skillet to the oven and bake for 20-25 minutes, until the chicken is fully cooked and the cheese is melted and bubbly.
7. Garnish with fresh basil and serve with pasta or a side salad.

Stuffed Bell Peppers

Ingredients:

- 4 bell peppers, tops cut off and seeds removed
- 1 lb ground beef or turkey
- 1 cup cooked rice
- 1 can diced tomatoes (14.5 oz)
- 1 small onion, chopped
- 1 clove garlic, minced
- 1 teaspoon oregano
- 1 teaspoon basil
- Salt and pepper to taste
- 1 cup shredded cheese (cheddar or mozzarella)
- Olive oil for cooking

Instructions:

1. Preheat the oven to 375°F (190°C).
2. In a skillet, heat olive oil over medium heat. Add onion and garlic, and sauté until softened.
3. Add ground meat to the skillet and cook until browned. Stir in diced tomatoes, oregano, basil, salt, and pepper. Simmer for 5 minutes.
4. Stir in cooked rice and remove from heat.
5. Stuff the bell peppers with the meat and rice mixture, packing tightly. Place them in a baking dish.
6. Top with shredded cheese and bake for 25-30 minutes, until the peppers are tender and the cheese is melted.
7. Serve hot, garnished with fresh herbs if desired.

Teriyaki Chicken and Veggies

Ingredients:

- 4 boneless, skinless chicken breasts
- 1 cup teriyaki sauce
- 1 tablespoon honey
- 1 tablespoon soy sauce
- 1 teaspoon sesame oil
- 1 teaspoon garlic, minced
- 1 teaspoon ginger, minced
- 1 cup broccoli florets
- 1 red bell pepper, sliced
- 1 zucchini, sliced
- 2 tablespoons vegetable oil

Instructions:

1. In a small bowl, whisk together teriyaki sauce, honey, soy sauce, sesame oil, garlic, and ginger.
2. Marinate the chicken breasts in the sauce for at least 30 minutes.
3. Heat vegetable oil in a large skillet over medium-high heat. Cook the chicken for 6-8 minutes per side, until browned and cooked through.
4. Remove the chicken from the skillet and set aside. Add the broccoli, bell pepper, and zucchini to the skillet, and cook until tender, about 5-7 minutes.
5. Slice the cooked chicken and return it to the skillet with the vegetables. Pour the teriyaki sauce over the top and toss to coat.
6. Serve hot, garnished with sesame seeds and green onions if desired.

Pot Roast

Ingredients:

- 3 lb beef chuck roast
- 4 carrots, peeled and cut into chunks
- 3 potatoes, peeled and cut into chunks
- 1 onion, chopped
- 3 cloves garlic, minced
- 2 cups beef broth
- 1/4 cup red wine (optional)
- 2 teaspoons rosemary
- 1 teaspoon thyme
- Salt and pepper to taste
- 2 tablespoons olive oil

Instructions:

1. Preheat the oven to 325°F (163°C).
2. Season the roast with salt, pepper, rosemary, and thyme.
3. In a large Dutch oven, heat olive oil over medium-high heat. Brown the roast on all sides, about 4-5 minutes per side.
4. Add garlic and onion to the pot and sauté for 2-3 minutes.
5. Add beef broth, red wine (if using), carrots, and potatoes to the pot. Bring to a simmer.
6. Cover and transfer the pot to the oven. Roast for 3-4 hours, until the meat is tender and falling apart.
7. Slice the pot roast and serve with vegetables and the pan juices.

Chicken Fajitas

Ingredients:

- 4 boneless, skinless chicken breasts, sliced into strips
- 1 onion, sliced
- 1 red bell pepper, sliced
- 1 green bell pepper, sliced
- 1 teaspoon chili powder
- 1 teaspoon cumin
- 1 teaspoon paprika
- 1 teaspoon garlic powder
- Salt and pepper to taste
- 2 tablespoons vegetable oil
- Tortillas for serving
- Lime wedges and fresh cilantro for garnish

Instructions:

1. In a small bowl, combine chili powder, cumin, paprika, garlic powder, salt, and pepper.
2. Toss the chicken strips with the spice mixture until evenly coated.
3. Heat vegetable oil in a skillet over medium-high heat. Cook the chicken for 5-7 minutes, until browned and cooked through. Remove and set aside.
4. In the same skillet, add the onion and bell peppers. Cook for 5-7 minutes, until softened and slightly charred.
5. Return the chicken to the skillet and toss with the vegetables.
6. Serve the fajitas in warm tortillas, garnished with lime wedges and fresh cilantro.

Beef and Vegetable Stir Fry

Ingredients:

- 1 lb flank steak, thinly sliced
- 1 cup broccoli florets
- 1 carrot, julienned
- 1 bell pepper, sliced
- 1/2 onion, sliced
- 2 tablespoons soy sauce
- 2 tablespoons oyster sauce
- 1 tablespoon sesame oil
- 2 cloves garlic, minced
- 1 teaspoon ginger, grated
- 1 tablespoon vegetable oil

Instructions:

1. In a bowl, whisk together soy sauce, oyster sauce, sesame oil, garlic, and ginger.
2. Heat vegetable oil in a large skillet or wok over medium-high heat. Add the beef and cook for 2-3 minutes until browned. Remove and set aside.
3. In the same skillet, add broccoli, carrot, bell pepper, and onion. Stir fry for 4-5 minutes until tender.
4. Return the beef to the skillet and pour the sauce over the top. Toss to combine and cook for an additional 2 minutes.
5. Serve hot with steamed rice.

Slow Cooker Pot Roast

Ingredients:

- 3 lb beef roast (chuck or brisket)
- 4 carrots, peeled and cut into chunks
- 3 potatoes, peeled and cut into chunks
- 1 onion, chopped
- 3 cloves garlic, minced
- 1 cup beef broth
- 1/4 cup red wine (optional)
- 1 tablespoon Worcestershire sauce
- 1 teaspoon thyme
- 2 bay leaves
- Salt and pepper to taste

Instructions:

1. Season the beef roast with salt, pepper, thyme, and bay leaves.
2. Place the roast in the slow cooker and add carrots, potatoes, onion, and garlic.
3. Pour beef broth, red wine (if using), and Worcestershire sauce over the roast.
4. Cover and cook on low for 7-8 hours or high for 4-5 hours, until the meat is tender and easily shreds.
5. Remove the roast and vegetables from the slow cooker. Slice the meat and serve with the vegetables and gravy.

Stuffed Cabbage Rolls

Ingredients:

- 1 large head of cabbage
- 1 lb ground beef
- 1/2 cup cooked rice
- 1 onion, chopped
- 2 cloves garlic, minced
- 1 can diced tomatoes (14.5 oz)
- 1/2 cup tomato sauce
- 1 teaspoon paprika
- 1 teaspoon thyme
- Salt and pepper to taste
- 2 tablespoons olive oil

Instructions:

1. Bring a large pot of water to a boil. Carefully remove the cabbage leaves and blanch them for 2-3 minutes. Set aside to cool.
2. In a skillet, heat olive oil over medium heat. Add onion and garlic, and sauté until softened. Add ground beef and cook until browned.
3. Stir in rice, paprika, thyme, salt, and pepper. Remove from heat.
4. Place a spoonful of the meat mixture in the center of each cabbage leaf and roll it up, tucking in the sides.
5. Place the stuffed cabbage rolls in a baking dish. In a separate bowl, mix together diced tomatoes and tomato sauce. Pour over the cabbage rolls.
6. Cover with foil and bake at 350°F (175°C) for 45 minutes.
7. Serve hot, garnished with fresh herbs if desired.

Chicken and Sausage Paella

Ingredients:

- 1 lb chicken thighs, boneless and skinless, cut into pieces
- 1 lb sausage (chorizo or smoked sausage), sliced
- 1 onion, chopped
- 1 red bell pepper, chopped
- 2 cloves garlic, minced
- 1 cup short-grain rice (such as Arborio or Bomba)
- 1 1/2 cups chicken broth
- 1/2 cup dry white wine (optional)
- 1 can diced tomatoes (14.5 oz)
- 1 teaspoon paprika
- 1/2 teaspoon saffron threads (optional)
- 1 teaspoon thyme
- 1/2 cup frozen peas
- 1 lemon, cut into wedges
- Olive oil for cooking
- Salt and pepper to taste

Instructions:

1. In a large, deep skillet or paella pan, heat olive oil over medium-high heat. Add the chicken and sausage, cooking until browned, about 5-7 minutes. Remove from the pan and set aside.
2. In the same pan, add the onion, bell pepper, and garlic. Sauté for 3-4 minutes until softened.
3. Stir in the rice, paprika, saffron (if using), and thyme. Cook for 2 minutes to toast the rice.
4. Pour in the chicken broth, wine (if using), and diced tomatoes. Bring to a simmer and then lower the heat. Return the chicken and sausage to the pan and stir.
5. Cover the pan and cook for about 20-25 minutes, or until the rice is tender and the liquid is absorbed.
6. Add the frozen peas, stirring them in. Cover and cook for an additional 5 minutes until heated through.
7. Serve the paella with lemon wedges for squeezing over the top.

Shrimp Scampi Pasta

Ingredients:

- 1 lb shrimp, peeled and deveined
- 8 oz linguine or spaghetti
- 3 cloves garlic, minced
- 1/4 cup white wine (optional)
- 1/2 cup chicken broth
- 1/4 cup lemon juice
- 1/2 teaspoon red pepper flakes (optional)
- 1/2 cup unsalted butter
- 1/4 cup chopped fresh parsley
- Salt and pepper to taste
- Olive oil for cooking

Instructions:

1. Cook the pasta according to package instructions, then drain, reserving 1/2 cup of pasta water.
2. In a large skillet, heat olive oil over medium heat. Add the shrimp and cook for 2-3 minutes per side until pink and cooked through. Remove from the skillet and set aside.
3. In the same skillet, add butter and garlic. Sauté for 1-2 minutes until fragrant.
4. Pour in the white wine and chicken broth, scraping any bits from the bottom of the pan. Let it simmer for 3-4 minutes until the sauce has reduced slightly.
5. Add the lemon juice, red pepper flakes, and salt and pepper to taste.
6. Return the shrimp to the skillet and toss to coat in the sauce. Add the cooked pasta and toss again, adding reserved pasta water if needed to loosen the sauce.
7. Garnish with parsley and serve immediately.

Beef Wellington Casserole

Ingredients:

- 1 lb ground beef
- 1 lb puff pastry (store-bought or homemade)
- 1/2 lb mushrooms, finely chopped
- 1/2 onion, chopped
- 2 cloves garlic, minced
- 1/2 cup beef broth
- 1/4 cup heavy cream
- 2 teaspoons Dijon mustard
- 1/4 cup fresh parsley, chopped
- 1 egg, beaten (for egg wash)
- Salt and pepper to taste
- Olive oil for cooking

Instructions:

1. Preheat the oven to 375°F (190°C). Grease a baking dish.
2. In a large skillet, heat olive oil over medium heat. Add the ground beef and cook until browned. Remove from the skillet and set aside.
3. In the same skillet, add the onion, garlic, and mushrooms. Cook for 5-7 minutes until softened and most of the liquid from the mushrooms has evaporated.
4. Stir in the beef broth, heavy cream, and Dijon mustard. Cook for 3-4 minutes until the mixture thickens. Season with salt and pepper.
5. In a large bowl, combine the cooked beef, mushroom mixture, and chopped parsley.
6. Roll out the puff pastry and cut it into pieces large enough to line the bottom of the baking dish and cover the top. Place the beef and mushroom mixture into the dish and cover with the puff pastry, sealing the edges.
7. Brush the top of the pastry with the beaten egg.
8. Bake for 25-30 minutes until the pastry is golden brown and puffed. Let rest for 5 minutes before serving.

Turkey Chili

Ingredients:

- 1 lb ground turkey
- 1 onion, chopped
- 1 bell pepper, chopped
- 2 cloves garlic, minced
- 1 can diced tomatoes (14.5 oz)
- 1 can kidney beans, drained and rinsed
- 1 can black beans, drained and rinsed
- 1 cup chicken broth
- 1 tablespoon chili powder
- 1 teaspoon cumin
- 1 teaspoon paprika
- Salt and pepper to taste
- Olive oil for cooking
- Sour cream and shredded cheese for garnish

Instructions:

1. In a large pot, heat olive oil over medium heat. Add the onion, bell pepper, and garlic, cooking for 4-5 minutes until softened.
2. Add the ground turkey and cook until browned, breaking it up with a spoon.
3. Stir in the chili powder, cumin, paprika, salt, and pepper.
4. Add the diced tomatoes, kidney beans, black beans, and chicken broth. Bring to a simmer.
5. Let the chili simmer for 30-40 minutes, stirring occasionally, until thickened and flavors meld together.
6. Serve hot, garnished with sour cream and shredded cheese.

Ratatouille

Ingredients:

- 1 eggplant, diced
- 1 zucchini, diced
- 1 yellow squash, diced
- 1 bell pepper, diced
- 1 onion, chopped
- 2 tomatoes, chopped
- 2 cloves garlic, minced
- 1/4 cup olive oil
- 1 teaspoon dried thyme
- 1 teaspoon dried basil
- Salt and pepper to taste
- Fresh basil for garnish

Instructions:

1. Heat olive oil in a large skillet or Dutch oven over medium heat. Add the onion and garlic, sautéing for 3-4 minutes until softened.
2. Add the eggplant, zucchini, yellow squash, and bell pepper. Cook, stirring occasionally, for 10-12 minutes until the vegetables begin to soften.
3. Stir in the tomatoes, thyme, basil, salt, and pepper. Cook for an additional 15-20 minutes until all vegetables are tender and the mixture is well combined.
4. Serve hot, garnished with fresh basil.

Beef and Cheese Taco Skillet

Ingredients:

- 1 lb ground beef
- 1 onion, chopped
- 2 cloves garlic, minced
- 1 packet taco seasoning mix
- 1/2 cup water
- 1 can diced tomatoes (14.5 oz)
- 1 can corn, drained
- 1 cup shredded cheddar cheese
- 1 cup sour cream
- Salt and pepper to taste
- Olive oil for cooking
- Chopped cilantro and lime wedges for garnish

Instructions:

1. In a large skillet, heat olive oil over medium-high heat. Add the ground beef and cook until browned. Drain any excess fat.
2. Add the onion and garlic to the skillet, cooking until softened, about 3-4 minutes.
3. Stir in the taco seasoning and water. Add the diced tomatoes and corn, then simmer for 5-7 minutes until the mixture thickens slightly.
4. Sprinkle shredded cheddar cheese on top and let it melt into the beef mixture.
5. Serve the taco skillet with a dollop of sour cream, chopped cilantro, and lime wedges.

Chicken Marsala

Ingredients:

- 4 boneless, skinless chicken breasts
- 1/2 cup all-purpose flour
- 1/2 cup olive oil
- 1 cup sliced mushrooms
- 3/4 cup Marsala wine
- 3/4 cup chicken broth
- 2 tablespoons butter
- Salt and pepper to taste
- Fresh parsley, chopped for garnish

Instructions:

1. Season the chicken breasts with salt and pepper, then dredge in flour, shaking off any excess.
2. In a large skillet, heat olive oil over medium-high heat. Add the chicken breasts and cook for 4-5 minutes per side, until golden brown and cooked through. Remove from the skillet and set aside.
3. In the same skillet, add the sliced mushrooms and cook for 2-3 minutes until tender.
4. Pour in the Marsala wine and chicken broth, scraping up any browned bits from the bottom of the skillet. Bring the mixture to a simmer.
5. Return the chicken to the skillet and cook for 5-7 minutes, allowing the sauce to reduce slightly.
6. Stir in the butter until the sauce is smooth and glossy.
7. Serve the chicken Marsala with the sauce and garnish with fresh parsley.

Sausage and Sauerkraut

Ingredients:

- 4 sausages (such as bratwurst or kielbasa)
- 2 cups sauerkraut, drained and rinsed
- 1 onion, sliced
- 1/2 cup beer or chicken broth
- 1 tablespoon mustard (optional)
- 1 tablespoon olive oil
- Salt and pepper to taste

Instructions:

1. Heat olive oil in a large skillet or Dutch oven over medium heat. Add the sausages and cook until browned on all sides, about 8-10 minutes. Remove the sausages from the pan and set aside.
2. In the same pan, add the onion and cook for 3-4 minutes until softened.
3. Stir in the sauerkraut, beer or chicken broth, and mustard (if using). Bring to a simmer.
4. Return the sausages to the skillet, nestling them into the sauerkraut. Cover and cook for 20-25 minutes, or until the sausages are fully cooked and the flavors have melded.
5. Serve the sausages with sauerkraut on the side.

Beef Burrito Bowls

Ingredients:

- 1 lb ground beef
- 1 onion, chopped
- 2 cloves garlic, minced
- 1 packet taco seasoning mix
- 1/2 cup beef broth
- 1 can black beans, drained and rinsed
- 1 cup cooked rice (white or brown)
- 1 cup shredded lettuce
- 1 tomato, chopped
- 1/2 cup shredded cheese
- 1/4 cup sour cream
- Salsa and guacamole for topping

Instructions:

1. In a skillet, cook the ground beef over medium-high heat until browned. Drain any excess fat.
2. Add the onion and garlic, cooking until softened, about 3-4 minutes.
3. Stir in the taco seasoning and beef broth, simmering for 5 minutes until the mixture thickens.
4. Assemble the burrito bowls by layering rice, seasoned beef, black beans, lettuce, and tomato in bowls.
5. Top each bowl with shredded cheese, sour cream, salsa, and guacamole.

Chicken and Rice Casserole

Ingredients:

- 4 boneless, skinless chicken breasts
- 1 cup uncooked rice
- 1 can cream of mushroom soup (or any cream soup)
- 1 cup chicken broth
- 1/2 cup shredded cheese (cheddar or mozzarella)
- 1/2 cup frozen peas
- 1 tablespoon olive oil
- Salt and pepper to taste
- Fresh parsley for garnish

Instructions:

1. Preheat the oven to 375°F (190°C).
2. In a large oven-safe dish, mix the rice, cream of mushroom soup, and chicken broth. Season with salt and pepper.
3. Place the chicken breasts on top of the rice mixture and drizzle with olive oil. Cover the dish with foil.
4. Bake for 40-45 minutes, or until the chicken is fully cooked and the rice is tender.
5. Remove from the oven, stir in the peas, and sprinkle with shredded cheese. Return to the oven for 5-10 minutes, or until the cheese is melted and bubbly.
6. Garnish with fresh parsley and serve.

www.ingramcontent.com/pod-product-compliance
Lightning Source LLC
LaVergne TN
LVHW061956070526
838199LV00060B/4143